ABC

POSITIVE AFFIRMATIONS

for Young Black & Brown Girls

by Aaliyah Wilson

Young Black and Brown girls should wake up and go to bed feeling empowered each day. This rhyming ABC story has encouraging words and affirmations from A all the way to Z to inspire girls and remind them of their

INNER STRENGTH, BEAUTY, POWER, AND WORTH!

A is for Afro

With pride in my roots, I love my textured coiled crown,
I will keep my head held high so it can never fall down.
I am proud of my curly hair,
I give it all of my love and all of my care.

B is for Beauty

I have an abundance of beauty from my body, to my skin,
and my glowing heart that I have right within.
I radiate beauty from the inside out!
Of that, I will never doubt.

C is for Confidence

I am confident enough to stand up for what I believe,
and when I do all things with confidence,
there is nothing I cannot achieve.
I believe in myself every step of the way,
from morning to night, every day.

D is for Dreams

I will make my dreams a reality, I will and I can!
I can accomplish all of the dreams that I plan.
I will be successful because I believe in me,
and I can become all that I want to be.

E is for Education

I am bright, I love learning, and I am so smart too!
Educating myself I always will do.
For my education, people of my history paved the way,
and I will honor them by learning something new each day.

F is for Freedom

I am free to be anyone I choose; I believe it to be so!
I am on Earth to flourish and grow.
I help others gain the freedom to be
the best they can become,
to better our world for generations to come.

G is for Greatness

I will unlock the greatness that was designed for me,
I will strive to be the best that I can possibly be.
I am thoughtful and I am kind,
I lift others up and I have a mighty strong mind.

H is for History

I am proud of my ancestors that came before me,
they taught me that I have the power to be free.
I appreciate the history and the struggle from long ago,
it shaped who I am today and allows me to grow.

I is for Inner Strength

I am capable, I am strong!
Wherever I go I take my strength along.
I can conquer any hardship and even if I fall,
I will gather my inner strength to rise and stand up tall!

J is for Jewel

I am as rare and as precious as a jewel,
I will always remember my value,
that's the number one rule.
Like a jewel, I sparkle and shine so bright,
I give to the world around me my glowing light.

K is for Knowledge

The more knowledge that I know,
the more that I can grow.
I seek the knowledge that is all around,
everywhere I look, there is knowledge to be found.

L is for Leader

I am a leader and I lead with grace,
I am on a journey to lead the world
to become a better place.
I will lead others around me on a path that is right,
because I am both powerful and bright.

M is for Miracle

I am a miracle and I am grateful to be alive!
In this world of opportunities, I will thrive.
Even when I feel lost, I will always find my way,
it is a blessing to wake up,
I will make the most of each day.

N is for Natural

I love my natural hair, beauty, and skin,
I love all that I am and the body that I'm in.
I love my curves and every inch of me,
I am the girl that I was always meant to be.

O is for Open-Minded

I will always go through life with an open mind,
there is a world of experiences and information to find.
I will show kindness and compassion to all,
and I will grow from new challenges, big or small.

P is for Pride

I am proud of my accomplishments and what
I've accomplished so far,
I give myself permission to shine like a star.
I am proud of my history, background, and experience too,
I show my pride in all that I do.

Q is for Queen

I am a queen and I will always remember
the power that I hold,
I am tenacious and I will always be bold.
I am elegant and as graceful as can be,
and I will strive to create the best version of me.

R is for Roots

I am thankful for my roots and from where I came,
I will honor my background which I am proud to claim.
I was created to be someone marvelous and great,
and I am destined for the future life I will create.

S is for Skin

My perfectly-colored skin is full of beauty and shine,
and I am happy that this wonderful skin is all mine.
It protects me from the sun's radiant shine,
my skin glows so beautifully and divine.

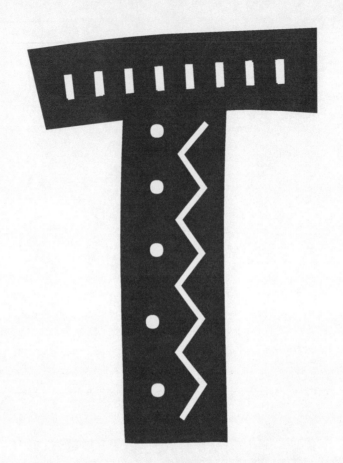

T is for Talented

I am talented, I am capable, there is nothing I can't do,
I am great at anything that I put my mind to.
I can achieve great success, I am outstanding in fact,
no matter what I choose to do, I am one great act.

U is for Unique

I am special and I am unique as can be,
there is no one else that is quite like me.
I am proud of the person that I become each day,
and I will remember how amazing I am
every step of the way.

V is for Voice

I will use my voice to speak out loud,
standing up for myself and others
will always make me proud.
I will use words that are impactful and true,
because words can change the world,
and that's what I'll do!

W is for Worthy

I am just as worthy as anyone else may be,
I deserve to be happy, loved, and to be free.
I belong anywhere that I choose to go,
and I allow myself the space that I need to grow.

X is for Extraordinary

I will dare to be different and extraordinary too,
making my presence known, I surely will do.
I am proud of myself and the words that I say,
and no one can take my specialness away.

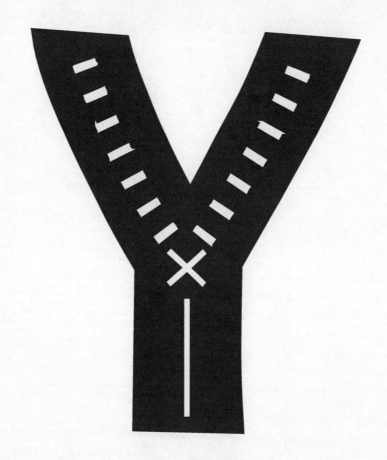

Y is for Yourself

Always be yourself, there is no better you around,
you are one of a kind and oh so profound.
You were meant to have enough joy and love to share,
your positivity radiates right through the air.

Z is for Zest

I will have a zest for the life that I live,
and every chance I can, I surely will give.
I will walk with my chin held high,
with confidence in my step, warmth in my heart,
and a twinkle in my eye.

Made in the USA
Las Vegas, NV
22 October 2023